FLOWERS
IN THE
HOME

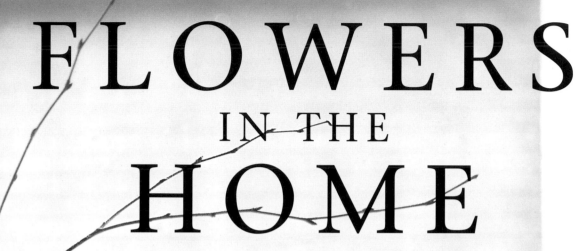

FLOWERS
IN THE
HOME

MARK UPTON

Introduction by JANE PACKER

SC
SH VEOHAD C IE BB VK TL MK

hamlyn

12.95

CONTENTS

Just what is it that inspires a floral designer to forsake a nice warm home in the early hours of a cold wet winter morning to go to market, and to do the equivalent of half a day's work while most people are still tucked up cosily in bed? It's a question I have often pondered as I return to my shop to face a day that will not finish any earlier than any other working person's, despite that early start.

INTRODUCTION

The answer is invariably at hand. Few things can match the thrill of unpacking and preparing the flowers ready for a day's trading, and being overwhelmed by the excitement of opening the first box of spring blooms flown in from warmer countries or seeing the rich beauty of foliage from great English country estates, with their deeply coloured berries and assorted leaf patterns. But this is not all: there is the constant pleasure of working with beautiful things and trying to present them as beautifully as possible.

When I began working with flowers as a Saturday girl at a small, local, family-run flower shop outside London, the varieties of flowers that were available were far fewer than is the case today and although I felt so fortunate (and still do) to be surrounded by such beauty and freshness I was very aware that what we were offering to our customers was sadly very limited. I couldn't understand why the flowers that my father grew in his garden simply were not available commercially. Also, flowers were generally purchased only for 'occasions', such as an anniversary gift, for a wedding or as a funeral tribute. It was rare for someone to buy flowers to brighten up their home; this was

considered extremely self indulgent.

The art of flower arranging was also hide-bound and static. It was ready for a change. Too many flower arrangements were statuesque and contrived, looking like poorly conceived sculptural studies. To be fair, this was not only the fault of florists. The general public didn't demand anything new from us and it was easier to turn out the same old tried and tested designs. The industry was 'comfortable' and although standards were definitely improving, this was within the confines of established and traditional ideas.

Thankfully that has all changed during my time in the industry and I have witnessed a revolution in this respect. Today things are different, people do buy flowers for themselves, and on a regular basis too. Many supermarkets include flowers among their normal range of produce, making them more accessible to most people, and although the current range of flowers they offer may sometimes be limited, it is growing rapidly. With an ever-increasing selection of blooms and foliage available, the hunger for whatever is new is constantly growing as well.

The neat and carefully balanced designs of the past are in merciful retreat, giving way to a look that is freer and more dynamic. This does not mean gathering a handful of flowers and just plonking them in a jam jar (although undoubtedly this can sometimes work), but what it does mean is not so readily defined.

I am one of that breed of people whose minds are constantly going off elsewhere. My attention is caught by an object and I am off. I see an antique vase and I start imagining its life story, wondering who has owned it, whether it was a gift, whether it has had sad associations. This quality has served me well in working with flowers since to keep one's ideas fresh, one must be open to inspiration from unusual sources, perhaps a creeper on the side of a house, a magazine advertisement, or the trees in a park. I went through a period of a particular fascination with vegetables, their shapes, colours and textures. They gave me new ways of looking at flowers and sometimes I could not resist including them in arrangements.

If my first impulse was to break away from the rigid designs used in traditional flower arranging, it was important to use that freedom to do the unusual and the novel. There is little point in abandoning one way of doing things just to get locked into another. The key is to use flowers and foliage as their character, colour and setting indicates, so that they do not appear contrived or forced. However, this does not mean avoiding any props other than a vase and water. Some experts denounce the use of florist's equipment like foam and chicken wire, but these can in fact help us achieve what we want without appearing false. The key thing is the appearance of the flowers – they must look right.

One element that receives too little attention is the smell of flowers, possibly because scent, in the past, has taken third place to colour and shape amongst growers. However, the scent of flowers can be apparent long before the flowers can be seen. Here again the occasion can be relevant, wonderful though the scent can be, it will interfere with the smell of food on a dinner table or with the bouquet of wine at a tasting. It can also hang too heavily in a confined space, such as a small bedroom.

Anyway, what started as means to earn a bit of pocket

money developed into a fascination with and lifelong love of flowers. I couldn't believe what could be done with flowers and how much detail, passion and pure hard work were involved in their preparation. It was inevitable that I would want to develop this passion through my career and bring my love of flowers to anyone who would listen.

As I have already said, a very large variety of flowers are now readily available, relatively inexpensively, from a magnitude of outlets, supermarkets being just one of them. Gone are the days when large chains 'threw in' a few plastic buckets of flowers at the checkouts along with the chocolates in the hope that they would attract an impulse buy. It is now realised that flowers play a much more important part in our lifestyles.

When I first opened my shop in London's West End fifteen years ago, I would cut flowers from my garden and the hedgerow to sell in an effort to rid the floristry industry of the reputation that it had earned itself for being 'fuddy duddy' by providing its customers with stiff and formal flower arrangements. I would introduce a little wildness and spontaneity to the flower arrangements that we produced and made a conscious effort not to associate my business with the rigid triangle approach to creativity that dominated the profession.

I was lucky enough to strike a chord with my customers and with the help of like-minded magazine stylists and editors, we were ready to introduce flowers as part of a contemporary lifestyle and nurture a new impression of the flower industry through magazine articles and books that featured flowers as part of the interior, in any room in the house. Thankfully, this approach was overwhelmingly adopted, an increasing number of flower retailers responded and this encouraged the growers to produce more and more varieties at a price that was commercially viable. This has led to a positive spiral of demand that continues to work in producing an ever-increasing availability of different flower varieties and colours. Many of those flowers that I was forced to pick from my own garden and the hedgerow are now grown commercially.

I would like to think that I have, in my approach to flowers, encouraged this movement and helped to redefine the role of the florist. I have been criticised in the past by people in the floristry business for 'going over to the other side' in helping large multiples develop their range of flowers for sale. The point is of course that the more people who are encouraged to buy flowers, the bigger the market gets, and the appreciation of the skill of the professional florist grows with this. During my career I have worked in all areas of the flower industry, and I have often found a reticence among my colleagues to share their skills and information with the public. Some florists feel that by selling florist's foam to customers and showing them how to arrange flowers, they may endanger their own livelihood. I believe this attitude is wrong. To encourage people to arrange flowers and to experiment with and enjoy the many varieties available means they will buy more flowers, demand different varieties, and expect longer-lasting and better-conditioned blooms. This has to be good both for the flower industry – an industry I feel

passionately about – and the customer who enjoys flowers.

It was the demand by non-professionals who were eager for more knowledge and information that led to the opening of my flower school ten years ago. During this time I have met many people who have a wonderful eye for colour and a real love of flowers, but who are desperate for more information and guidance on what to do with flowers. They long to escape from the rigid, formal teaching that many have experienced with traditional exponents of "floral art" to a more realistic approach. They come to my school because they want to achieve with flowers a look that is natural, uncontrived, and easy to live with. These ideas embody my philosophy of flower arranging, and I have aimed to teach them in my school.

I have been lucky, I've met and worked with many talented people over the years who have shared my belief that flowers should play a positive part in our lifestyle, a

part of our home, not obvious but subtle, always there, a part of our environment.

But what's really exciting about this is the opportunity to fuel an ever increasing appetite … the next new flower. Longiflorum Lilies and Sunflowers have been re-invented. Like food with its many variations on a regional theme, new strains of flowers and variations on traditional varieties are coming to the fore. Through my shops, school, and my work with many major companies (fashion, food, perfume), I like to think that our varied experiences help lead us and point us in the 'right' direction, indeed our customers rely on us to get it just right. The influences that we thrive on come from many different sources and of course I don't operate alone, I am part of a team.

I was very lucky when I first opened the school to be working with a very talented lady, Jane Yianni, who helped me set up the school and was the principal tutor in those early years. When she left London for the pleasures of the countryside another talented colleague, Tracey Gallaccio, took over the reins but sadly she was also forced to retire.

I have always been fortunate to have had the pleasure of employing creative and committed individuals. When the position of the head tutor of the school was available, I knew that Mark Upton was the perfect choice, and he took on the challenge with relish. Now a full director on our company board, the success of the school and the need to move to larger premises is a testament to his skills and enthusiasm.

I've had the pleasure of working with Mark Upton for many years now, and during this time I've seen a lot of books on flower arranging published. However, no one, I believe, deserves more than Mark to have his work, talent and style captured within a book.

Mark has a natural ability to make something look just right, whether it's a single bloom or a more lavish combination. It is his eye for detail that is often demonstrated, choosing the right container that enhances the shade or shape of the flowers with no great song or dance about it. He makes it look easy. Through our work together teaching at my school, the comment we most often hear from a student is frustration felt by many that the flower displays

often featured in magazines or books by other so-called 'flower designers' are unaffordable, using a mass of glamorous obscure flowers that are virtually non existent twenty miles outside London! This book is not like that. Mark and I share a belief that less is often more, and teach that one single beautiful vase of flowers can say more than something three times its size.

It is with this philosophy in mind that Mark has approached this book. He has shown flower displays that everyone can attempt and achieve. They are made from flowers that are available and also affordable and if an expensive variety has been used then it is in an idea that uses it sparingly. The simple yet so clever combinations of flowers and vases featured make this book a 'must have' for the thousands of people who love to have flowers in their homes, buy them regularly and enthusiastically, then struggle when it comes to the arranging bit. Struggle no more, it doesn't have to be difficult. Mark has made it easy, just as it should be!

Jane Packer

The brightest colour in the spectrum, with warmth and luminosity, yellow is fun. From tiny Primroses in early spring to the sophisticated Calla Lily, yellow flowers are vivid and dramatic.

YELLOW

Daffodils simply strewn in a jug epitomise spring and help ward off those harsh winter days. If you want to lighten a dark hallway, add yellow flowers for impact and a warm welcome is assured.

sunflower topiary

SUNFLOWERS HAVE INCREASED hugely in popularity and availability over recent years. When I first started working in floristry, they were a flower that was rarely, if ever, seen for sale commercially. Today they are a familiar flower in the supermarket or florist shop and are grown in many countries, including Spain, Israel and even good old England. I decided to fashion these into a topiary tree, which has become a popular style. You will need about ten stems for this arrangement.

IN THE BEGINNING

First remove all the foliage – although this may seem criminal, the weak appearance of the leaves doesn't look good for very long.

IN SHAPE

Hold the flower heads close together to form a spherical shape, with the straighter stems to the centre and the arching stems to the outside edges. Bind the bunch firmly together with string or a rubber band. Cut all the stems to the same level.

STEM SUPPORT

I've chosen a yellow enamel bucket to contain the flowers, which are standing in a glass of water effectively concealed by six lemons. The additional flower at the base adds extra interest and helps to support the tree and keep it upright.

FOCAL POINT

Finally, scatter more lemons around the bucket or place it next to a bowl of the same fruit so the arrangement links visually with its surroundings. This is the perfect display to put in a kitchen or living room, and creates an interesting focal point.

grouping containers

GROUPING CONTAINERS TOGETHER on different levels creates a more spontaneous effect. Here I've selected a 1950s -inspired yellow trophy vase and a shot glass. The differing shades of yellow work together well and sit tidily on the windowsill. I have used a minimal amount of material. Sometimes I think it can be disappointing when 'florists' or 'floral designers' overstuff arrangements with masses of different flowers. I think each element should be seen and add a special significance.

STEM SUPPORT

Sunflowers are available for much of the year but I enjoy them most in the summer. There are many different types available commercially; although this type with the black eye is the easiest to find.

IN SHAPE

This style of vase can often be seen in churches with tall spikes of gladioli, chrysanthemum sprays and carnations arranged in a perfect triangle. However, this sensually shaped vase needs very little decoration as its shape is so beautiful. I've cut three sunflower heads short and rested their heads on one side of the vase to create an asymmetrical design.

FOCAL POINT

This yellow rose is a commercially grown variety called 'Golden Times' and it helps to continue the colour theme. I could perhaps have selected a garden rose and arranged it in a similar way, for I love selecting a specially nurtured bloom from the garden.

Variation

Always add a bit of foliage with a rose as this helps it to look more natural.

calla lilies

CALLA LILIES SHOULD BE CONSIDERED a luxury. They are usually quite an expensive purchase, but they look so wonderful that they can be regarded as a sound investment – in other words, money well spent in terms of the enormous pleasure that they give in return. Related to the Arum Lily, *Zantedeschia atheopica* or Easter Lily, these mini versions are an absolute delight.

IN SHAPE

The flowers seem almost to resemble a cone of paper and are absolutely fantastic to arrange.

Variation

As an alternative to Calla Lilies try using tall spikes of Gladioli in the same way, which will create a bold, dramatic statement. If you cannot find any trailing Ivy, perhaps raffia or a knot of fabric could be tied around the vase to introduce further interest.

IN THE BEGINNING

I used a glass vase to show off the arching stems. Trails of Ivy are wound into a circle. The lower stem should have its leaves removed and be placed beneath the water level, securing the circle of foliage around the rim of the vase.

STEM SUPPORT

I've used berried Tree Ivy, which will form a base and help to support the flower stems. If a stem arches in a particular direction, try to exaggerate this tendency when you position it. This will achieve a natural-looking design.

chrysanthemum heads

WHY IS IT THAT CHRYSANTHEMUMS are so often rubbished so quickly by so many supposed flower gurus? I couldn't disagree with them more. I think that Chrysanthemums are great and that, like most flowers, they can look absolutely fantastic if they are given just a little special loving care and attention to detail. Chrysanthemums are the number one, top-selling cut flower.

IN THE BEGINNING

Chrysanthemums last a really long time and should be teamed up with an interesting container which emphasizes their colour. Choose a sympathetic foliage and you will be heading for a more distinctive arrangement.

STEM SUPPORT

Here I've saved a couple of broken heads from an arrangement that I had already made and teamed them with a sprig of yellow variegated Ivy in a yellow shot glass tumbler. A simple, quick, yet effective arrangement.

rising ranunculus

THE RANUNCULUS IS RELATED to the Buttercup family and is a flower that is both delicate and long lasting. Different varieties are available in a wide range of colours, from September until May – both as cut flowers and as pot plants. The bowl-shaped flowers have a great many petals, which can often be stroked back gently to exaggerate their size.

FOCAL POINT

I've chosen two simple test tube bases to decorate a window ledge. The flower stems have been cut at slightly different levels, which adds a little spontaneity to the group. Simple test tube vases work most effectively with one ingredient. Choose architectural forms such as Tulips, Gerbera, Lilies and Antirrhinums.

Variation

As an alternative to these arrangements, you could try sprigs of Catkin twigs, Icelandic Poppies or even more exotic sprays of Orchids.

tulips and twigs

TULIPS ARE AVAILABLE as a cut flower for much of the year now, from September right through until June. I think, however, that it seems a little sad that all the seasons have got mixed up. Here I've used a variety called 'Yokohama', which is easily obtainable and a rich vibrant colour. Tulips are a flower with a particularly strong form and work well if arranged simply.

IN THE BEGINNING

Here I've teamed them up with a yellow enamel bucket, some Birch twigs, raffia and moss to create a very natural-looking arrangement.

IN SHAPE

Place some florist's foam in the container and cover with rich verdant moss. Push the flower stems through the moss into the foam beneath. The flowers have deliberately been cut at different lengths so that they actually appear to be growing.

STEM SUPPORT

The Birch twig fence acts partially as a decoration but is also used to support the flower stems.

FOCAL POINT

As Tulips age, the stems lengthen and the flowers respond to gravity – I enjoy it when this happens as it's the natural response of the flower. I've bundled together some of the remaining twigs and bound them together with more raffia. Add further sprays of twigs to heighten the arrangement and to create a natural impression. Cut the fence posts and supports at clean angles, as this will improve the overall finish of the design. Remember to 'top up' the florist's foam daily with fresh water.

sunshine group

TO CREATE AN INTERESTING DISPLAY, it's a good idea to combine a variety of containers of different heights, textures and shapes. Here I have selected a black vase, and have wrapped it with yellow wool. The wool is firmly anchored into position with double-sided sticky tape.

IN THE BEGINNING

The lower vase is a simple shiny ceramic pot, but it could equally well be a jug or a mug from the kitchen. Nothing can escape its own potential for being used as a vase.

STEM SUPPORT

Solidago, or 'Golden Rod', is a wonderful bushy plume-like flower. I've taken three stems and cut them short to form an outline shape. This is then embellished with three stems of the Lily, 'Connecticut King'.

IN SHAPE

The second pot is just filled with Achillea or Yarrow. The heads have been levelled together and form a pleasingly rounded dome shape that makes you want to reach out and touch them.

FOCAL POINT

I decided to leave the black
stamens in place, as they link
wonderfully well with the rim
of the string-covered pot.
But beware – Lily pollen can
stain clothes and furnishings
quite badly.

Bright and fresh, clean and classical, white flowers are very useful for creating a minimalist modern look. White flowers for me seem to epitomise sophistication.

WHITE

I have found immense inspiration from the white garden at Sissinghurst, designed by Vita Sackville-West in the 1950s. She was a true visionary, with a great understanding of colour.

planted azaleas

AZALEAS ARE LONG-LASTING flowering plants, which require regular watering and should not be allowed to totally dry out. The easiest watering method is to totally immerse the pot under water until the bubbles stop. The pot should then be full of water, which the compact root system will appreciate. You can check the weight of the pot daily as a watering guideline.

IN THE BEGINNING

The flowers' slightly green tinge works effectively with variegated trailing Ivy.

STEM SUPPORT

I've chosen a limed wooden container and a selection of seashells. Line the container with plastic and support the plants in position with Sphagnum Moss. Allow the trailing Ivy to spill downwards and break the edges of the container.

IN SHAPE

The shells create a decorative finish and disguise the pot tops and Sphagnum Moss. As alternatives you could select cones, gravel or pebbles. The two scallop shells placed overlapping at the base of the container help to settle the arrangement into its location.

arums and twisted hazel

FOR A REALLY SPECIAL OCCASION, it's great fun to decorate your home and to create an attractive and eye-catching focal point. The glass trumpet vase is pleasingly simple in both line and shape, and complements the equally simple conical shape of the flower absolutely perfectly.

STEM SUPPORT

Begin by arranging the twisted Hazel. It will be helpful to split the stem end vertically with scissors so that it can drink up the water easily.

STEM SUPPORT

When you add the Arum Lilies, start with the tighter flowers toward the outside edges first. Imagine that you are extending the cone of the vase upwards. The curved stems should flare out from the vase and it's fun to exploit the plant's naturally curving stems.

IN SHAPE

Place a more open flower head towards the centre of the arrangement. This will create a central point, which will help to give a sense of visual stability to your arrangement.

FOCAL POINT

It is a good idea to arrange larger vase displays like this in their final location as you can adjust the stem lengths to suit the area you are decorating and ensure that the design fits its location. Here the flowers are framed by the curtains.

mini white gerbera

GERBERA ARE A CONTEMPORARY and fun flower. They are available in a huge range of colours. They are a very versatile flower and work effectively either arranged in a mass, or simply placed in individual specimen vases. The possibilities are endless and much is left to your personal style and imagination. They can be used to decorate every room in the house, including the smallest room.

IN SHAPE

I've massed together several mini-Gerbera to create a rounded cushion effect and popped them into a chrome toothbrush beaker.

FOCAL POINT

Alternatively, you can decorate a mirror with these versatile test tube vases. They are fun, spontaneous and relaxed.

Variation

Tulips, Anemones or Orchids would work well as alternative flowers in these test tube vessels.

white amaryllis

HIPPEASTRUM ORIGINATE FROM SOUTH AMERICA and are commonly sold as Amaryllis. They can be grown from a bulb or purchased as a cut flower from September until March. They are often expensive as a cut flower but well worth the investment as they last well. Here I've selected just two white stems and put one in each vase for a simple yet modern effect.

FOCAL POINT

Amaryllis are grown from large bulbs with strap-shaped green leaves. The stout, hollow flower stem bears several trumpet-shaped flowers, which are available in shades of red, pink, white and yellow.

There's something exciting about the first green shoots in the spring time. Green is often considered a neutral colour, but it can be used with zest and imagination. Green flowers are rare.

GREEN

'Shamrock' is a Chrysanthemum that has become popular lately as lime has become such a good colour for the interior designer. I am pleased that Chrysanthemums are getting a look-in again.

group of jugs

INSPIRATION COMES FROM a great many different directions – some of them surprising and unexpected ones. Here, this wonderful cabbage leaf pottery plate set me on my way, raiding the kitchen cupboards in search for alternatives to the more usual, typical flower vase. My solution was to select a co-ordinating variety of white and cream jugs, which perfectly pick out the leaf veins of the pottery.

IN THE BEGINNING

Always ensure that the container is really clean and fill the jug with clean fresh water. Sometimes if you use a particular vessel regularly, bacteria will soon develop, which can dramatically diminish the lasting time of the flowers.

FOCAL POINT

In this situation, the mood of the arrangement should be casual and informal – almost country style, in fact. I've chosen a selection of green flowers and foliage. Berried Tree Ivy hangs on the left, while lime green Bupleurum is massed to the right. Spiky stems of Amaranthus take a central back position, with a frilly Ornamental Cabbage creating a focal point.

IN SHAPE

Lighter material works well towards the outside edges of the arrangement while heavier or more open flowers look good centrally. The setting of jugs has been completed by the final addition of a 'Mind-your-own-business' plant in the smaller cabbage pot. It fits perfectly and appears to bubble gently over the edge of the container like a pan of boiling milk.

shamrock chrysanthemums

CHRYSANTHEMUMS ARE NATIVE TO China and Japan. I've decided to allow this to influence my arrangement, which is, as a result, strongly Oriental in feel. I've added a subtle twist of Willow for an extra Oriental touch. This casual little cluster of pleasant greenery could be used to extend a warm welcome to a visitor – perhaps in a guest bedroom or bathroom, say.

FOCAL POINT

Two similar vases of different heights and shape have been grouped together and a single bloom is plopped into each vessel. Ensure that the lower leaves have all been removed.

STEM SUPPORT

If the stem is particularly woody, cut a vertical split up the stem. This will ensure that the flower takes up water easily.

IN THE BEGINNING

The Chrysanthemum is such an interesting flower, with almost tactile appeal, that it is hardly surprising that it has become so popular.

Variation

For alternative Oriental-looking flowers, have a go with Orchids, Camellias or Antirrhinums. Look at patterned Oriental fabrics for further inspiration.

Some flower arrangers are wary of blue flowers because they think of blue as a cold colour, which can seem to disappear in a dark or shady environment. Give blue a try for a fresh, clean arrangement.

BLUE

There are some wonderful blue cut flowers available. Think of Bluebells, Grape Hyacinths and Violets in the spring, followed by fantastic spikes of Delphinium and large mopheads of Hydrangea.

glass tank with pebbles

A SIMPLE GLASS TANK is one of the most versatile containers that you can choose. It's neutral and will settle comfortably into a number of surroundings, whether traditional or modern. If you use the tank regularly for flowers, bacteria may start to develop in the corners of the vase, so make sure you wash it out regularly with bleach, as bacteria will prevent your flowers from lasting well.

IN THE BEGINNING

I've arranged each flower type in an individual group. This helps to encourage a natural look as each flower type feels like an individual plant. This means that the overall impact of each ingredient is stronger.

STEM SUPPORT

Try supporting stems within the vase with pebbles, rocks or marbles. Your choice should link with your selection of flowers and help to emphasise the colour theme.

IN SHAPE

In this arrangement, the silver grey pebbles work especially well with the tones of pale blue on silver, and create an interesting, watery, late summer design.

FOCAL POINT

Globe Thistles radiate from
one point, while a single head
of Hydrangea and a couple of
sprays of Eryngium complete
the design.

dark purple anemones

ANEMONES ARE A FAVOURITE FLOWER OF MINE because of their strength of colour. As a child I always remember being given a bunch of these during the Mother's Day service at our local church and presenting them to my mother with immense pride. Here I've decided to choose rich purple ones as I think these are the strongest colour of all, and have real power.

IN THE BEGINNING

I've gone for strength and simplicity here. Make up a line of containers and simply place an individual head in each drinking glass. Here I've used short blue recycled glasses.

FOCAL POINT

You could use this formal line-up in a number of different ways. It would look extremely good down the centre of a dining table, for example, or it could grace a mantelshelf, or – as here – a simple window sill.

IN SHAPE

It is amazing how much water Anemones will drink, so make sure that the glasses are topped up with water regularly. They are surprisingly thirsty little flowers.

Variation

Other blue flowers that would look effective given this treatment might be Muscari, or Grape Hyacinths, which are small and delicate and have a wonderful fragrance. However they can be difficult to find commercially but can be easily grown in the garden or window box.

agapanthus

AGAPANTHUS HAS A MEDITERRANEAN QUALITY for me, recalling sun-baked holidays in the south of France and in southern Spain. The long, elegant, arching stems can look very effective when they are arranged simply to give a strong modern effect.

Variation

This arrangement would look most effective positioned in a bright and open space such as a modern kitchen or bathroom.

IN THE BEGINNING

First of all, you should select an appropriate container. Here I wanted to exaggerate the length of the stems, so I opted for a tall, narrow-necked ceramic vase. This proved to be the perfect choice.

STEM SUPPORT

When you arrange the individual flowers, ensure that there is enough space around each stem. First arrange stems around the outside edge of the container and then fill in the centre with additional stems.

IN SHAPE

I have deliberately kept every item the same length. This mimics the way the plant grows naturally and creates a simple contemporary look. I do not feel that it is necessary to add any foliage here as it might well confuse and detract from the pleasing simplicity of the flower heads.

blue hyacinths

HYACINTHS ARE VERY POPULAR flowers and herald the early spring. They are available in cream, white, and various shades of pink and blue. These highly scented flowers can make a room smell – as well as look – absolutely delicious. They can be bought both as cut flowers and as potted plants, and can be tremendous fun to grow yourself from the bulbs.

IN THE BEGINNING

For this arrangement, I've selected a few rather major ingredients to complement the 20 stems of Hyacinth. The large glass bowl has been partially filled with pumice stone pebbles. Next, a central candle was inserted and carefully, but firmly, wedged into position.

Variation

As an alternative, Tulips could be used for this design.

STEM SUPPORT

Taking individual stems of these gloriously blue Hyacinths, arrange the flowers around the candle in the centre of the arrangement, and following the edge of the bowl.

FOCAL POINT

Where possible, it is a good idea here to exaggerate any naturally arching stems so that they act as a gentle break against the edge of the container.

Pink flowers can often look a little on the sickly and gooey side, rather like cheap shop-bought cakes. However, if they are used carefully, they can also look light and dreamy.

PINK

I've tried to show a variety of ideas with pink flowers. Pale pink double Angelica Tulips, shocking pink Jacaranda Roses and mopheads of glossy Hydrangea are just three of my favourites.

pink basket

THIS SMALL BOTTLE BASKET was a useful find and came in very handy. It is divided into six equal compartments and makes a delightful container. I decided to fill three of the compartments, each with a different type of flower. I put glasses of water in the containers first. I deliberately chose contrasting shades of pink flower. I used a soft steel pink Bouvardia, tall and spiky Antirrhinums, and rounded bowl-shaped Ranunculus, with a rich abundance of petals.

IN THE BEGINNING

Insert clean glasses of water into the basket and cluster together one flower type in each vessel, as this will help to maximise the overall impact.

IN SHAPE

The Bouvardia and Ranunculus have been kept deliberately low and to the same side. The taller spikes of Antirrhinums are positioned to the opposite side of the basket.

FOCAL POINT

The three remaining compartments of the basket could then be filled with home-made sweets or cosmetics. This would make a special Mother's Day gift of distinction.

Variation

As the compartments of this basket are fairly small, an abundance of material is not really necessary. Precious clippings from the garden could look equally effective for an informal look. Consider herbs such as Rosemary or Purple Sage. A green variety of Hellebore called 'Corsica' looks great with sprigs of Catkins for a springtime basket design.

coal bucket of lilies

THE GALVANISED COAL BUCKET is a strong and imposing container so needs to be complemented with a sympathetic combination of flowers and foliage. I have selected the heavily scented 'Stargazer' lily with a variety of foliage to complement.

IN THE BEGINNING

Ensure the bucket is filled with clean deep water. You could also add a bit of flower preservative to help feed the flowers and prolong their life.

STEM SUPPORT

Berried Ivy is dark green with a dark brown berry, which links with the table top. The cascade of Eucalyptus has a reddish stem which enhances the colour of the flowers, and the silver leaves work well with the metal of the container.

The remaining foliage helps the flowers to stand out as both contain yellow which adds brightness. I selected variegated Golden Privet and Bupleurum, a common commericial variety.

IN SHAPE

I have grouped the foliage in sections to maximise its impact. Distribute the flower stems evenly, pushing them through the foliage. The material should hold their position well. A smaller bowl contains a broken Lily stem. The hanging Eucalyptus stems unite the containers.

Variation

Large galvanised buckets or even cooking pots can look beautifully decadent when filled with one flower type en masse. In the springtime try ten bunches of daffodils or in early summer a plethora of pink peonies.

single flower simplicity

SOMETIMES LESS REALLY CAN be more. Here I've added a single Gerbera to a test tube vase to decorate the window sill. The pale pastel pink looks great against the light blue sky. There are many other flowers that could work well given this treatment.

IN THE BEGINNING

Make sure you choose a clean and bold form for a contemporary look. Try a Latin Dahlia or a sophisticated Calla Lily. As an alternative to this container, you could select a tall thin bottle, which would exaggerate the narrow line of the window.

carnation topiary

TRY MAKING A CARNATION TOPIARY to give this traditional flower a thoroughly modern twist. An unexpected treatment of many flowers can work surprisingly well. Topiary trees can work well with many other flowers, too. Paper white Narcissi, for example, smell absolutely divine, while Anemones in mixed colours have a rather more casual, rustic charm, which would look especially good in a breakfast room, an informal dining room or a kitchen.

FOCAL POINT

As a container, I was lucky to find a '50s-style plastic beaker, which is a particularly successful choice as the Carnations themselves also seem to evoke memories of that particular era.

IN SHAPE

Level the flower heads to form a spherical shape and fasten with ribbon, cord or string. Tie this into a casual bow, trim the stem ends all to the same length, and stand them in a cup of water.

sophisticated orchid

THE MOTTLED PINK PHALAENOPSIS or Moth Orchid is an expensive purchase, but should prove to be a worthwhile investment as the flowers last for a good couple of weeks. The plant requires a warm and humid environment and will re-flower if it is given a good resting period during the winter months, and a regular liquid feeding programme in the springtime.

Variation

For alternative contemporary plants try sophisticated Arum Lilies, strong and architectural Amaryllis bulbs or bright and extremely vivid Gerberas in clashing colours.

IN THE BEGINNING

The branch of twisted Hazel is a perfect choice here. It looks slightly unexpected and helps to exaggerate the exotic theme of the arrangement. The Hazel branch is carefully pushed downwards between the plants.

IN SHAPE

Orchids make up the second largest plant family. Although many varieties can be difficult to look after, there are several varieties which can survive in living rooms. A humid environment is essential with good ventilation and protection from direct sunlight.

FOCAL POINT

The galvanised, semi-circular wall-hanging container makes an ideal holder for the Orchid, which is carefully nestled into position and surrounded by trailing Ivy plants and mosses. I have used two silver mosses here: trailing Spanish Moss and Lichen, or Reindeer Moss, which, both being in shades of grey and silver, complement the tin container perfectly. The ladder to the left is from Thailand and helps to continue the exotic travel theme.

Mixing colours can create bold and striking dramatic arrangements. Inspiration for flower colour combinations can come from a great variety of different sources.

MIXED COLOURS

I've found inspiration from gardens, trips abroad, fruit and vegetable markets, and even from clashing jumpers stacked neatly in clothes shops. Go on, be daring, have fun and experiment.

red and blue arrangement

TO CREATE THIS RICH BOWL ARRANGEMENT I have made a vibrant selection of materials. Red and purple Anemones work together perfectly and look opulent when teamed with red Ranunculus and delicate Hypericum berries. I have decided to arrange this selection in a shallow glass bowl. In order to support all the stems safely I will use some sticky tape to make a grid across the container. You will find that the network of leafy stems will easily support the top-heavy seedheads and hold them firmly in place.

STEM SUPPORT

When attaching the tape, ensure the tip of the container is dry. The size of the grid will be determined by the size of the flower stems you choose. For example, thicker flower stems like Amaryllis or Delphiniums may require a bigger grid.

BASIC OUTLINE

Begin by making an outline shape with the Hypericum berries. I've clustered together three sprigs levelled to a similar height. The overall arrangement is kept low and rounded, as this will give maximum impact.

BASIC OUTLINE

Group together areas of red and blue flowers – so the finished design resembles a patchwork. Smaller buds of Ranunculus have been used to soften the edges of the bowl and help to increase the natural look of the design.

rustic trug

THIS INFORMAL PLANTED BASKET would brighten up a balcony or roof terrace as all of these plants are quite hardy and will tolerate cooler temperatures. Alternatively it would liven up a hallway or garden room. However make sure it is watered regularly and has plenty of light but not direct sunshine.

IN THE BEGINNING

Heather or Erica plants bring feathery splashes of colour in white, purple and shades of pink. Here I have selected some different shades for additional interest.

BASIC OUTLINE

Ivy is a wonderfully useful and tolerant plant to grow which enjoys being clipped every so often. These clippings could be used for fresh flower arrangements, so it's worth stocking several types in your garden.

FOCAL POINT

There are hundreds of varieties of Ivy or Hedera with a different size and shape of leaf.

Variation

There is a huge range of variegations with colourings which will vary enormously from lime green, yellow and dark green and white.

pink, purple and silver

SELECTING THE CORRECT CONTAINER for your chosen flowers is half the battle. Wide-necked vases will obviously require greater quantities of flowers and narrow-necked vessels are helpful for supporting arching stems such as tulips. Food or bowls can be grouped with vases to continue or extend your theme. They can be filled with fruit, pebbles, shells, sand or even floating flower heads.

BASIC OUTLINE

Freesia is in the top ten list of the most popular selling cut flowers and the reason is likely to be its strong perfume. This variety 'Cote d'Azur' is particularly bold and strong and looks good with the blue and silver vase.

STEM SUPPORT

Here I grouped together two contemporary-looking vases of different heights. The extra silver platter and bowl help to continue the theme. I've used shocking pink raffia, too, and tied it around the neck of the lower vessel containing a rounded mass of Freesia.

FOCAL POINT

Tulips look most effective when arranged en masse. This allows the arching stems to fall elegantly over the edge of the vase and radiate out from the centre of the container. I especially enjoy the way tulips respond to gravity as their stems continue to grow.

Variation

Flower petals could be floated in the remaining bowl. Springtime cherry blossoms would create a wonderfully decadent effect, even if just casually scattered around the arrangement.

Bright, zesty and radiant, orange
flowers add a warming glow.
There is a wealth of subjects to
choose from: Euphorbia,
Physalis and Marigolds are just
three of my favourites.

ORANGE

Orange often suggests autumn,
and there are several fruits and
vegetables that can be combined
to emphasise this seasonal theme.
Oranges, pumpkins and peppers
can all add fun and vibrancy.

window pots and chillies

PERHAPS FOR BONFIRE NIGHT or for a Hallowe'en party, it could be a lot of fun to try this simple, quick, yet highly effective idea. The bright orange colour scheme has been chosen to fit the theme, but also helps to create a festive atmosphere. Three terracotta pots have been tied parcel-fashion with raffia. This acts partly as a decoration but also helps to support the flowers firmly in position.

IN SHAPE

Chillies are available as a cut flower and are imported from Italy. If you can't get hold of this orange variety, try fresh red or green chillies from the supermarket for an alternative colour theme.

Variation

As an alternative, try making similar garlands of cherries. The pots contain blood-red garden roses.

IN THE BEGINNING

First prepare your garlands. I've chosen natural raffia but garden twine or wool could look equally effective. Knot individual heads of chilli to the raffia at irregular intervals and hang at different heights.

IN SHAPE

Finally, to settle the arrangement in position, surround the pot with more raffia and scatter another chilli garland. This enhances the informal look of the arrangement.

birds of paradise

STRELITZIA ARE TENDER BRIGHTLY COLOURED PLANTS whose flowers resemble the head of a bird with a bright orange crest splashed with inky blue. They are extremely long lasting flowers and grow readily in hot climates. When it is available, the silver grey paddle-like foliage of the Strelitzia can be fun to arrange, too, and helps the flowers to feel a little more at home.

BASIC OUTLINE

Eucalyptus is a wonderfully useful foliage which is readily available throughout the year. It grows very vigorously and the new growth can be trimmed from an established tree about twice a year. It is an essential plant for the keen flower enthusiast. I've used several stems to create an attractive base.

STEM SUPPORT

Strelitzia can be delicately prised open and the sticky lower spikes splayed out. Here I've used five flower stems and positioned the heads so they radiate out from the centre of the foliage.

FOCAL POINT

Ensure there is space around each bloom. I've used a wooden container here which doesn't in fact hold water. Lurking under the foliage is a glass vase filled with water. I think the silver colour of the rounded leaves of the Eucalyptus works beautifully with the bird of paradise flowers of the Strelitzia.

tulip simplicity

ALTHOUGH TULIPS ARE traditionally a spring flower, they are commercially available for much of the year. It should be noted, however, that they are at their strongest and sturdiest when the temperature is naturally cool – namely from January until April. Here I've opted for a simple and strong look, selecting flowers of one single variety, called 'Admiral Rembrandt'.

Variation

A strong contemporary look can easily be achieved by selecting a quantity of one flower type. For large imposing displays try vases of Gladioli, Ornamental Onion Flower or Amaryllis.

IN SHAPE

The tulips have been arranged in a simple glass vase, which helps to show off their arching flower stems. Tulips continue to grow while they are in water, and the stem will also respond to light and gravity. Often people are disappointed that tulips droop very quickly. To avoid this, ensure they have had a good drink before arranging them. You can do this by wrapping them tightly in newspaper and placing them in deep water. Always remember to trim the stem ends at an angle if the flowers have been out of water for some time, as this will enable them to drink more quickly.

STEM SUPPORT

The tulips have been spiralled so the stems all follow the same direction. To achieve this effect, place each stem at the same angle from left to right. Hold the bunch at one point and rotate it regularly, adding stems at the same angle each time. Keep the flower heads softly domed in shape and place more arching stems towards the outside edges. Trim all of the stems to a similar length. The glass vase works effectively for these 'Admiral Rembrandt' tulips as its narrow neck helps to support the stems and perfectly shows off the spiral and the arching stems.

hallowe'en table setting

FORTUNATELY, THE DAYS OF formal dining are fast disappearing. It's fun that flowers, food, china and the surrounding area can all be linked together through your choice of materials and ingredients. Here I've combined pumpkins, oranges, napkins and wooden containers, and have achieved a contemporary and stylish table setting.

IN THE BEGINNING

Gerbera have become a very popular cut flower, available in a huge colour range and variety of types throughout the year.

FOCAL POINT

I think that the days of the static table arrangement made on florist's foam or oasis have gone. Leave behind anything that looks like it's been turned out of a mould and go for something more dynamic and fun, which is what I've tried to do here. I've selected just six stems, using a simple test tube vase supported in a block of birch wood. Cut the flower heads at different heights and face each flower head in a different direction, looking out from the centre of the table. Cluster together heavier objects towards the centre of the table and use brighter, lighter flowers towards the edges.

This is a classic colour for romance. The top-selling Rose is a red one. Other red flowers which create a sense of drama and luxury are Gladioli, Anemones, and even Carnations.

RED

Rose growers have produced some wonderful red varieties. Look out for 'Nicole', 'Grand Prix' and 'Baccarole' – three top-of-the-range Roses which are well worth buying for a special anniversary.

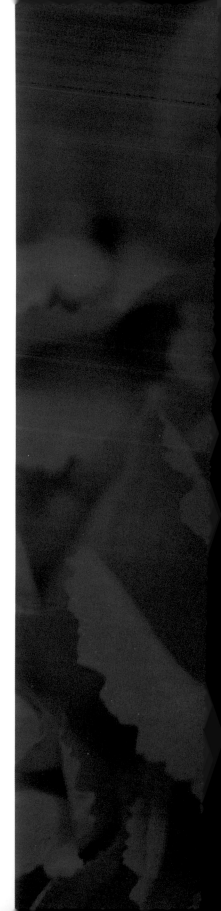

gerbera topiary tree

GERBERA ARE BRIGHT AND MODERN flowers which work well when they are clustered together tightly to form a topiary tree arrangement. To underline the contemporary theme, I've selected a glass cube or tank vase. Glass is a wonderful material because it is neutral and does not fight with its surroundings. As an alternative container a galvanised bucket topped with moss would achieve a similar effect.

IN THE BEGINNING

To start, prepare your container by popping a glass of water in the tank and surrounding it with some raffia – here I've chosen red raffia. Fruit, nuts or even shells would be effective, too.

IN SHAPE

I've gathered together about 15 stems. Try to keep the shape rounded, and secure the bunch with a knot of raffia tied high under the necks. Cut the stems to a similar length and, to finish, add a shorter stem at the base of the trunk. Check the water daily.

FOCAL POINT

A topiary tree is very versatile and can look good in a variety of different surroundings. It can emphasise a contemporary ambience, for example, or it can blend well with a traditional style of interior.

Variation

This design can be made with a variety of other flowers. Try paper white Narcissi for a delicately scented floral tree. Mixed coloured Anemones can look fun, too, or for something bright and funky, see the Sunflower topiary on page 12.

red lilies with twigs

MONTENEGRO LILIES are a long-lasting variety which has a tendency to open fairly quickly. This can be useful if you need a quick splash of colour to brighten your living room. Here I've incorporated the six Lilies with a selection of twigs and some lime green Bupleurum to give the red a kick. Lime green is a fantastic colour for adding brightness and useful, too, for bringing out the colour of other materials.

IN THE BEGINNING

The neutral ceramic vase has been wrapped with twigs. Adding twigs to the arrangement gives height and additional interest.

STEM SUPPORT

Thread an elastic band over the vase, then push stems of twig under the band all the way around the vase. Allow the branches to reach up around the lip of the vase. First position twisted Willow twigs in the vase to create height. Thread the lime Bupleurum through the twigs. Cut it to a similar height to create a stronger impression. Evenly space the Montenegro Lilies through the Bupleurum. Make sure there is space around each flower. Remove the leaves from a trail of Ivy and wrap it around the vase several times to cover the band.

Variation

You could cover a vase with many other materials. For Christmas, try a few sticks of cinnamon. For a fresh effect, try large green Laurel leaves. Or to co-ordinate with your table, wrap an ugly container with cloth napkins and tie with wool, rope or raffia.

christmas table setting

RED IS A TRADITIONAL COLOUR for Christmas. Here I've teamed together fruit, flowers, foliage, crockery and candles to create a table setting of distinction. Table centres can look as if they have been turned out of a mould but, fortunately, the days of formal tables are becoming a thing of the past. Allow flowers, foliage, fruit and candles to take over the table so the overall look feels spontaneous and opulent. The trailing Ivy, sprayed with gold paint, creeps from the central vase and winds across the table, twisting between plates and glasses of wine – thus stylish, decadent dining is assured.

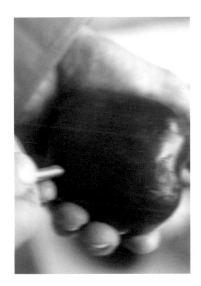

STEM SUPPORT

The apples have been securely anchored on Rose stems. Simply push a stem or kebab stick into the fruit so that it enters the core of the apple and then arrange away.

IN SHAPE

The Roses should be added evenly throughout the container. Larger more open flowers work well towards the centre, while brighter buds look good towards the outside edge. This mimics a natural style – in nature, finer buds and branches of a tree are positioned to the outer edges, whereas the weight of the tree is towards the centre.

IN THE BEGINNING

When arranging the Roses, first prepare the Tree Ivy foliage. Create a base by cutting all stems to a similar length. Allow the berries to hang over the edge of the vase, to create a natural effect and exploit their pendulous habit.

FOCAL POINT

Tie napkins with additional trailing Ivy and scatter fruit. Alternatives are numerous – cones, cinnamon sticks, shells or moss – just remember to stick to a strong, bold theme and to co-ordinate with this throughout.

One of the qualities that I enjoy about flowers is their temporary and short, yet perfect, life. But many of us want a living arrangement that will stick around for some time and fill a dull space.

LONGER LASTING

People are often disappointed when cut flowers last only a few days. Here I hope to show you some plant and flower combinations that should last several weeks.

house plant selection

A PLANT CAN OFFER a different dimension to a room. Greenery in a small flat without an outside space, for example, can bring a fresh burst of vitality. However, select carefully and don't overdo it. There is nothing worse, in my opinion, than too many plants, so beware of African Violet families taking over the window sill or armies of Spider Plants creeping across the shelves.

IN THE BEGINNING

The silver tones of these cacti are enhanced by the zinc containers. Spanish Moss and pebbles which cover the compost add interest and are sympathetic with both plant and container alike.

FOCAL POINT

Spanish Moss is quite an interesting find. Not from Spain at all, it is, in fact, American and is found in swampy regions hanging from tropical trees. Here I have allowed it to escape a little out of the pot.

STEM SUPPORT

These Ficus benjamina, or Weeping Figs, have wonderful braided stems. The plants have been trained to grow in a topiary style and will stay like this if they are clipped into shape about twice a year. Three plants grouped together create a modern look. Threes, fives, nines – they all work well, depending on the available space.

mother in law's tongue

THIS PLANT IS EITHER LOVED OR LOATHED – I happen to like it. Sansevieria is one of those house plants that deserves a revival. The tall striped yet spiky leaves create a modern look. I enjoy this kind of fine attention to detail. One could similarly exaggerate a 1970s feel by the use of certain plants, such as a large leafed Philodendron, for example.

IN SHAPE

The grey pebbles that cover the compost link nicely with the metal lamp stand, too. The overall effect is strong and uncomplicated – great.

hydrangea design

ALTHOUGH QUITE A COMMON-OR-GARDEN PLANT, Hydrangea, for me is an essential flower to grow. Forced Hydrangea house plants with fantastic mopheads can be purchased from April until July and, once they have finished flowering indoors, they transfer well to the garden. Ensure your house plant receives plenty of water. Hydrangea is the Greek for water, which suggests that this species is one which enjoys plenty of moisture. For best results, totally immerse the pot beneath the water level until the bubbles stop.

BASIC OUTLINE

To make your arrangement feel part of the interior choose sympathetic elements which blend well together.

STEM SUPPORT

Here I've chosen a Chinese ceramic pot cover. As there's a hole in the bottom of the pot I've lined it with a pudding basin to hold water. An upturned drinking glass forms a plinth for the burgundy-coloured candle. You could wedge this into position with blue plasticine if you're worried that it may wobble. Surround the candle with several heads of Hydrangea. Adding some foliage from the plant as well helps to frame the flowers and separates the individual heads.

Variation

In the autumn Hydrangea which is growing outside reacts to temperature, changing the colour of the flower heads into wonderful burnished shades of red and claret.

TECHNIQUES

ALTHOUGH I FIND THE IDEA of flower arranging rules a little frightening, there are, it must be said, a few guide lines which can be followed to ensure your cut flowers last well and look distinctive. For me it is most important that the flowers and plants which you select for your home look comfortable and not over-contrived. It seems appropriate for today's hectic lifestyles that flowers look relaxed and spontaneous.

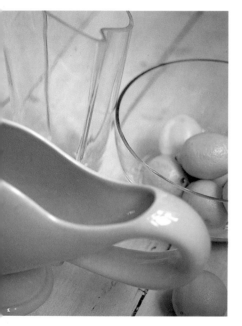

Always make sure the vase you select is really clean with no dirty blotches lurking in the corners.

Whenever you are given flowers or indeed purchase them yourself, ensure that before arranging them the stems are re-cut on an angle. Cutting stems at a clean, sharp angle allows a greater surface area for water to travel up the stems. Next give the flowers a good long drink in a deep bucket of water for at least two hours. If the flowers look particularly tired this is even more essential.

Flower food crystals, which are often supplied on many cut flower bunches from supermarkets, are well worth using, particularly when you are giving the flowers a long drink prior to arranging. Unfortunately the yellowish appearance of these crystals can look unsightly in a clear glass container but there is no problem with a ceramic one.

Always make sure that lower foliage is removed and that stems which are beneath the water level are clean. Leaves left underwater will encourage the build-up of bacteria, which may cause your flowers to die prematurely.

Woody-stemmed subjects such as Lilac, Chrysanthemum blooms and woody foliage like Eucalyptus and Golden Privet will appreciate their stems being split. Simply cut the stem vertically upwards. This encourages water to travel up the stem more effectively and unlike crushing with a hammer will not damage the stem which is sometimes quite delicate.

So that your flowers last well do not place them in direct sunlight. If the weather is particularly hot or the flowers drink quickly like anemones, for example, make sure you top up the vase regularly with fresh clean water.

Certain lily varieties, for example 'Stargazer' or 'Enchantment', carry pollen which may stain clothing or furnishings. This should therefore be removed to prevent accidents, although sometimes this seems a little harsh.

It is preferable to remove leaves by hand rather than cutting them off with scissors, as I think it destroys the look of the flower. Dead-heading older or lower blooms can be helpful as it will encourage further buds to open. Remove the larger dead heads from Freesia and the lower blossoms of Gladioli for example.

creating a theme

IT IS IMPORTANT that the flowers we select for our homes link visually with their surroundings and indeed the type of container used should be in keeping, too. Here I've selected two metal containers of different heights. This enables me to make a larger display and creates an informal effect.

The daisy motif on the vase is why I selected the cream Daisy Chrysanthemums. The silver foliage of Senecio works beautifully, too, with the containers. In the smaller vase I have removed several heads from stems of Chrysanthemum spray and teamed them with some variegated Golden Privet foliage. The arrangement has been deliberately left low and rounded and measures less than the height of the container. This maximises the impact of the flowers.

The taller vase contains stems of silver Senecio clipped from the garden to create a natural effect. Look carefully at each stem and try to exaggerate its curves and bends.

Silver vases work well in this modern chrome kitchen. Always try to link vases with their environment. If the room is heavily patterned, a neutral glass container will blend rather than clash with its surroundings.

AVAILABILITY

YELLOW

ACHILLEA	*FILIPENDULA 'MOONSHINE'*	April – September
CALLA LILY		October – May
CHRYSANTHEMUM	*DENDRANTHEMA 'GREEN PEAS'*	All year round
DAFFODIL	*NARCISSUS, 'GOLDEN HARVEST', 'CARLTON'*	December – April
LILY	*'CONNECTICUT KING', 'MONA'*	All year round
RANUNCULUS		October – May
ROSE	*'GOLDEN TIMES', 'COCKTAIL'*	All year round
SOLIDAGO (Golden Rod)		All year round
SUNFLOWER		All year round
TULIP	*'YOKOHAMA', 'GOLDEN APELDOORN'*	December – April

WHITE

AMARYLLIS	*'LUDWIG DAZZLER'*	September – March
ARUM LILY		All year round
CARNATION	*DIANTHUS 'DELPHI'*	All year round
GERBERA	*BIANCA*	All year round

GREEN

AMARANTHUS		June – September
BERRIED IVY		October – April
BUPLEURUM	*'GRIFFITHII'*	All year round
CHRYSANTHEMUM	*'SHAMROCK', 'SILVER DOLLAR'*	All year round
EUCALYPTUS	*'PARAFOLIA'*	All year round
HYDRANGEA		August – October
ORNAMENTAL CABBAGE		August – November

BLUE

AGAPANTHUS	*'DONAU'*	May – September
ANEMONE	*'MONA LISA'*	September – June
ECHINOPS	*'GLOBAL THISTLE'*	June – October
ERYNGIUM ALPINUM		June – September
FREESIA	*'COTE D'AZUR'*	All year round
HYACINTH	*'DELFT BLUE'*	December – April
HYDRANGEA		August – October

PINK

ANTIRRHINUM (Snapdragon)	*'MAJUS'*	All year round
BOUVARDIA	*'ROXANNE'*	All year round
CARNATION	*DIANTHUS 'MILADY'*	All year round
GERBERA MINI	*'TALENT'*	All year round
LILY	*'STARGAZER'*	All year round
RANUNCULUS		May – October
TULIP	*'BLENDA'*	December – April

ORANGE

CHILLIES		August – November
CHRYSANTHEMUM	*DENDRANTHEMA 'TIGER'*	All year round
GERBERA	*'CASINO'*	All year round
HYPERICUM	*'EXCELLENT FLAIR'*	All year round
ROSE	*'LAMBADA', 'PRALINE'*	All year round
STRELITZIA	*REGINAE*	All year round
TULIP	*'AD REM'*	November – April

RED

AMARYLLIS	*'RED LION'*	October – March
ANEMONE	*'MONA LISA'*	August – May
CARNATION	*DIANTHUS 'GIGI'*	All year round
GERBERA	*'CHATEAUX'*	All year round
LILY	*'MONTENEGRO'*	All year round
RANUNCULUS		May – October
ROSE	*'GABRIELLE'*	All year round

index

First published in the U.K. in 1998 by Hamlyn
an imprint of Octopus Publishing Group Limited
2–4 Heron Quays, London E14 4JP

Copyright © 1998 Octopus Publishing Group Limited

Distributed in the United States by Sterling Publishing Co., Inc.
387 Park Avenue South, New York, NY10016-8810

Printed in China

ISBN 0 600 59951 5

Picture Credits

Special photography by David Loftus
Styling by Mark Upton